AF486670

WIDERANGE GUIDE TO STARTING

A...

SIX-FIGURE REMODELING CONTRACTOR BUSINESS TODAY

BY

KEVIN STARKS
GENERAL CONTRACTOR &
FOUNDER OF CONTRACTOR ENVY

Copyright © 2023 Contractor Envy Publishing

All rights reserved. No part of this publication may be reproduced, distributed, or transmitted in any form or by any means, including photocopying, recording, or other electronic or mechanical methods, without the prior written permission of the publisher, except in the case of brief quotations embodied in critical reviews and certain other noncommercial uses permitted by copyright law. For permission requests, write to the publisher, addressed "Attention: Permissions Coordinator," at the address below.

ISBN: 978-8-89034-663-6 (eBook)

Any references to historical events, real people, or real places are used fictitiously. Names, characters, and places are products of the author's imagination.

Front Cover image and Book Design: Kevin I. Starks
Interior Layout and Typesetting: Indra Bahadur Rai
Printed: ,n the United States of America.

First printing edition 2023.

Published by:
Contractor Envy Publishing
6505 E Central Ave. Suite 285
Wichita, Kansas 67206

www.contractorenvy.com

TABLE OF CONTENTS

O P E N I N G

INTRODUCTION

"From Novice To Leader: The Inspirational Journey"

Starting a construction company from scratch can be a daunting task, especially for those who have no prior experience in the industry. But, as Kevin I Starks Sr. would tell you, it is not impossible. His story of starting a construction company within 15 minutes in a title company's parking lot is both compelling and intriguing.

For Kevin, it all started when he enrolled in a vocational course called Building Trades in 2011. Before that, he was just a guy who could use power tools and had no interest in the construction industry. But after completing the course, he found himself drawn to the world of construction. He learned the basics of plumbing and electrical, and it wasn't long before he put himself out there as a general contractor to his family and friends.

His first job as a general contractor came unexpectedly, when he was asked to manage some work to be done at an investor's rehab project. The scope of work included plumbing and electrical issues, which he was not qualified to handle himself. However, he knew he could get the work completed by someone in his network.

After gathering enough notes and information from the property managers, Kevin reached out to his trade contacts and was able to get a plumber and an electrician onsite to give him an estimate of what they would charge him to complete their scope. He was then able to take their estimates, add his markup, and send it over to the customer.

Even though Kevin did not have a way to send his estimate over to the client, he found an app on his phone that did invoices and estimates. His bid was sent over via invoice app within 48 hours, and he was able to mark up 100% considering the data he found for these two trades where the hourly rate was well over $100 an hour.

Despite the challenges of not having the proper business infrastructure in place, Kevin's first job as a general contractor was a success. He made $1,000 profit in just two days by managing the project while at his full-time job. This success gave him the motivation to pursue a career in the construction industry, and he has been able to achieve great things ever since.

Kevin's story proves that it doesn't take much to start a residential remodeling company. All you need is the first job, and you can grow from there. The key is to have persistency and to be able to communicate effectively with your customers.

If you are considering starting a contracting business such as a special trades, general contracting or project management business with no prior experience, Kevin's story is an inspiration. It shows that with determination, resourcefulness, and a willingness to learn, anyone can achieve success in the construction industry.

Pro tip:

Stop overthinking and start taking action towards your goal. Break down the overwhelming task of starting a business into smaller, manageable steps.

Go tip:

Take the first step today by researching your local regulations and requirements for starting a business. Look into obtaining any necessary licenses, permits, and insurance. Create a simple business plan outlining your goals, services, and target market. Start networking and building relationships with potential clients and industry professionals. Don't wait for the "perfect" moment, start today and keep moving forward.

1

TRANSFORM LIVES AND HOMES

Why Joining The Thriving Residential Remodeling Industry Should Be Your Next Move

The residential remodeling industry is a dynamic field that offers opportunities for people from various backgrounds. From carpenters to designers, the industry welcomes people with diverse skills and experiences. **Here are seven reasons why you should consider joining the residential remodeling industry today:**

Growing Industry: The residential remodeling industry is rapidly growing, and according to the National Association of Home Builders, it is projected to increase by 4.5% annually over the next decade. This growth will lead to an increase in demand for skilled workers and professionals.

High Demand: The demand for remodeling services is consistently high, as people continue to renovate and upgrade their homes. This means there will always be a steady flow of work, providing job security and a stable income.

Creative Freedom: The residential remodeling industry is a creative field that allows you to express your creativity and make a difference in people's lives. You can use your imagination and skills to create beautiful and functional living spaces that reflect your clients' personalities and lifestyles.

Career Growth: The industry offers excellent opportunities for career growth and advancement. You can start as a carpenter or painter and work your way up to become a project manager or designer. With hard work and dedication, you can build a successful and rewarding career in the industry.

Flexibility: The residential remodeling industry offers flexibility in terms of work schedule and location. You can work as a freelancer or start your own business, allowing you to have control over your work hours and the type of projects you work on.

Helping People: One of the most rewarding aspects of the residential remodeling industry is the opportunity to help people improve their living spaces. You can make a positive impact on people's lives by creating beautiful and functional living spaces that enhance their quality of life.

Financial Benefits: The residential remodeling industry offers excellent financial benefits, including competitive salaries and the potential for significant profits if you start your own business. Additionally, you can save money by working on your own home improvement projects.

In conclusion, the residential remodeling industry offers numerous opportunities for people who want to work in a dynamic, creative, and growing field. If you're passionate about making a positive impact on people's lives, improving living spaces, and creating beautiful and functional spaces, then the residential remodeling industry is the right fit for you. Join the industry today and start building a rewarding career.

Pro tip:

Network with industry professionals and seek out mentorship opportunities to gain insights and advice from experienced contractors. This can help you navigate common challenges and avoid costly mistakes.

Go tip:

Start small by taking on small projects and building your skills and reputation gradually. This can help you gain confidence and establish a solid foundation for your business. Additionally, consider taking courses or online training to improve your skills and knowledge in the industry.

2

UNLOCKING THE SECRETS

*How a Residential Remodeling Company
Works and How You Can Profit from It*

A residential remodeling company is a business that specializes in renovating or improving homes. These companies provide a wide range of services, including kitchen and bathroom remodeling, room additions, basement finishing, and outdoor living spaces. In this article, we'll discuss what a residential remodeling company does, how it makes money, and how you can start a successful remodeling business by following these same steps.

What does a residential remodeling company do?

A residential remodeling company works with homeowners to improve their homes by providing a wide range of services, including:

Kitchen and bathroom remodeling: This includes everything from updating fixtures and appliances to completely redesigning the layout of the space.

Room additions: This involves adding new rooms to an existing home, such as a new bedroom or home office.

Basement finishing: This involves converting an unfinished basement into a livable space, such as a family room or home theater.

Outdoor living spaces: This includes building decks, patios, and outdoor kitchens to enhance a home's outdoor living area.

How does a residential remodeling company make money?

Charging for services

The most straightforward way that a residential remodeling company makes money is by charging for their services. Companies typically charge an hourly rate or a flat fee for their services. Hourly rates are often used for small projects or for work that is difficult to estimate in advance, such as repairs. Flat fees are more commonly used for larger projects, where the scope of the work is better defined.

When charging for services, it is important for the company to accurately estimate the time and cost required to complete the project. This involves taking into account the cost of materials, labor, and any subcontractors that may be needed. Companies may also factor in a profit margin to ensure that they are making money on the project.

Marking up materials

In addition to charging for their services, residential remodeling companies may also mark up the cost of materials. This involves purchasing materials at a wholesale price and then charging the customer a higher price to cover the cost of the materials, as well as a markup for the company.

Marking up materials can be a lucrative source of revenue for a residential remodeling company, but it is important to do so fairly. Customers are often able to compare the cost of materials online, and if they feel that they are being overcharged, they may choose to take their business elsewhere.

Referral fees

Another way that residential remodeling companies can make money is by receiving referral fees from other companies. For example, a remodeling company may refer a customer to a flooring company for new hardwood floors. If the customer decides to use the flooring company, the remodeling company may receive a referral fee for the referral.

Referral fees can be a good source of income for residential remodeling companies, but it is important to be transparent with customers about any referral fees received. Customers may feel uncomfortable if they feel that the company is steering them towards a particular company solely for financial gain.

Upselling

Upselling is the practice of suggesting additional services or products to customers beyond what they originally requested. For example, a customer may ask for a new bathtub, but the remodeling company may suggest that they also replace the tile around the bathtub for a more complete look.

Upselling can be an effective way to increase revenue for a residential remodeling company, but it is important to do so ethically. The additional services or products suggested should be genuinely beneficial to the customer, rather than simply an attempt to increase revenue.

In conclusion, residential remodeling companies make money primarily by charging for their services and marking up the cost of materials. They may also receive referral fees and upsell additional services or products to customers. Ultimately, the success of a residential remodeling company depends on its ability to provide quality work and excellent customer service, as satisfied customers are more likely to refer the company to others and provide repeat business.

Pro tip:

To profit from residential remodeling, it's essential to manage your finances effectively. Keep track of your expenses and ensure that you are pricing your services competitively while still making a profit.

Go tip:

Research the current market rates for residential remodeling services in your area and compare them to your costs to determine your pricing. Develop a clear pricing strategy that factors in labor, materials, overhead costs, and a reasonable profit margin. This will help you to attract clients while ensuring that your business remains profitable. Additionally, consider offering incentives such as referral discounts or seasonal promotions to increase your business and profits.

BUILDING YOUR FUTURE

The Pros and Cons of Starting a Residential
Remodeling Business

Pros of starting a residential remodeling business

3 BUILDING YOUR FUTURE

The Pros and Cons of Starting a Residential Remodeling Business

Starting a residential remodeling business can be an exciting and rewarding venture. The opportunity to transform people's homes and bring their visions to life can be incredibly fulfilling, both creatively and financially. However, as with any business, there are both pros and cons to consider before taking the leap. In this article, we'll explore the benefits and drawbacks of starting a residential remodeling business.

Pros of starting a residential remodeling business:

Creative fulfillment: One of the most significant benefits of starting a residential remodeling business is the opportunity for creative fulfillment. Remodeling projects allow contractors to take a space and transform it into something beautiful and functional, using their skills and expertise to bring their clients' visions to life.

Financial potential: Residential remodeling can be a lucrative business, with the potential for high profit margins on projects. As homeowners invest in improving and updating their homes, the demand for remodeling services continues to grow, creating a steady flow of business for contractors.

Flexibility: Starting a residential remodeling business can provide a great deal of flexibility in terms of work schedule and location. Contractors can choose the projects they take on, allowing them to work on their own terms and take on as much or as little work as they choose.

Personal relationships: Residential remodeling projects often involve a great deal of personal interaction with clients, allowing contractors to build relationships with homeowners and become a trusted source of advice and expertise. This can lead to repeat business and referrals, helping to build a strong reputation in the community.

Variety of work: Residential remodeling projects can vary widely in scope and complexity, providing a wide range of opportunities for contractors to use their skills and creativity. This variety can help keep the work interesting and engaging, reducing the risk of burnout.

Cons of starting a residential remodeling business:

Startup costs: Starting a residential remodeling business can require a significant investment in tools, equipment, and materials. This can be a significant barrier to entry, especially for contractors who are just starting out.

Competitive market: The residential remodeling industry can be highly competitive, with many established players in the market. This can make it difficult for new businesses to stand out and attract clients, especially in areas where there are already many established contractors.

Seasonal demand: Residential remodeling projects can be highly seasonal, with many homeowners preferring to undertake renovations during the summer months. This can lead to uneven workloads throughout the year, making it difficult to plan and budget for business expenses.

Liability concerns: Residential remodeling projects can carry a high level of liability risk, as contractors are responsible for ensuring that their work is safe, up to code, and meets the expectations of their clients. This can result in potential legal and financial consequences if something goes wrong.

Client management: Residential remodeling projects can involve a great deal of personal interaction with clients, which can sometimes lead to difficult or demanding clients. Managing client expectations and resolving conflicts can be a significant source of stress for contractors.

Conclusion:

Starting a residential remodeling business can be a great way for contractors to use their skills and creativity to transform homes and build a profitable business. However, it also comes with its own set of challenges, including high startup costs, competition, seasonal demand, liability concerns, and client management. Before starting a residential remodeling business, it's important to carefully consider these pros and cons and develop a solid business plan that addresses these challenges. With the right strategy and approach, a residential remodeling business can be a successful and rewarding venture.

C H A P T E R

4

FROM ZERO TO HERO

Starting a Six-Figure Residential Remodeling Company with No Experience and What It Would Take

Starting a residential remodeling company with no experience can seem daunting, but it's not impossible. With hard work, dedication, and a willingness to learn, you can start your own business and build a successful career in the industry. In this chapter, we'll discuss what it would take to start a residential remodeling company with no experience.

Educate Yourself

The first step to starting a residential remodeling company is to educate yourself about the industry. This can include taking classes, reading books and articles, and attending industry events. By gaining knowledge and understanding about the industry, you can make informed decisions about your business and build a strong foundation for success.

Build a Network

Building a network of professionals in the industry is critical for starting a successful remodeling company. This can include architects, designers, contractors, and other professionals who can provide guidance and support as you start your business. Attend industry events, join local professional associations, and connect with professionals on social media to build your network.

Start Small

Starting small is essential for building a successful remodeling company. Begin by taking on small projects and building your reputation as a reliable and skilled professional. As you gain experience and build your network, you can begin taking on larger projects and expanding your business.

Invest in Quality Tools and Equipment

Investing in quality tools and equipment is essential for starting a successful remodeling company. You'll need a variety of tools, including saws, drills, hammers, and more, as well as equipment like ladders and scaffolding. Quality tools and equipment will help you complete projects efficiently and effectively, and will also help you build a positive reputation in the industry.

Focus on Customer Service

Customer service is critical for building a successful remodeling company. Focus on providing exceptional customer service to your clients, including clear communication, timely responses, and a commitment to delivering high-quality work. Happy clients are more likely to refer you to their friends and family, which can help grow your business over time.

Conclusion

Starting a residential remodeling company with no experience requires hard work, dedication, and a willingness to learn. By educating yourself, building a network, starting small, investing in quality tools and equipment, and focusing on customer service, you can build a successful remodeling company and establish yourself as a skilled and reliable professional in the industry.

Pro tip:

Start small and focus on one specific area of expertise to build your skills and reputation in the industry.

Go tip:

Reach out to established contractors in your network and offer to assist them on projects to gain hands-on experience and learn the ins and outs of the business. Also, take advantage of online resources and courses to gain knowledge on the industry and best practices for starting a successful residential contracting business.

5

RESIDENTIAL GENERAL CONTRACTOR VS. SPECIAL TRADES CONTRACTORS

Which One Fits Your Business Model?
Pros and Cons

Starting a business in the construction industry can be a profitable venture for entrepreneurs. One decision that new business owners in the construction industry must make is whether to start a specialized special trades business or a general contracting business. Both options have advantages and disadvantages, and it is important for entrepreneurs to weigh the pros and cons of each before deciding which one to pursue.

As a contractor, it's important to understand the differences between a residential general contractor and a special trades contractor. While both have similar goals of completing a construction project, their business models differ significantly.

A residential general contractor is responsible for overseeing the entire construction project. They handle the planning, budgeting, and management of the project, including hiring subcontractors and coordinating their work. A general contractor is responsible for ensuring that the project is completed on time, within budget, and to the satisfaction of the client.

On the other hand, special trades contractors specialize in a specific trade, such as painting, tile installation, drywall installation, or framing. They are typically hired by the general contractor to perform specific tasks within the construction project. Special trades contractors are skilled in their particular trade and can provide high-quality work in their area of expertise.

There are benefits to both business models. General contractors have a more diverse skill set and can manage the entire construction project. They have a better understanding of the big picture and can make informed decisions that benefit the overall project. They also have the opportunity to build relationships with clients and subcontractors, which can lead to future business opportunities.

Special trades contractors, on the other hand, have a more focused business model. They are experts in their particular trade and can provide high-quality work. They have lower overhead costs since they only need to focus on one trade, which can lead to a higher profit margin.

When deciding which business model to pursue, it's important to consider your strengths and weaknesses as a contractor. If you have experience in managing large projects and have a diverse skill set, becoming a residential general contractor may be the best fit for you. If you have a specialized skill and enjoy working on specific tasks, becoming a special trades contractor may be the best fit.

Specialized Special Trades Business:

A specialized special trades business focuses on a specific type of construction trade, such as painting, tiling, or drywall installation. These businesses typically hire skilled workers who specialize in one area of construction and have a high level of expertise in that area. Here are some of the advantages and disadvantages of starting a specialized special trades business:

Advantages:

Specialized skills: Special trades businesses offer specialized skills and knowledge in one area, which can result in a higher quality of work and a competitive edge in the market.

Lower overhead costs: Specialized special trades businesses often require less overhead costs as they don't have to invest in equipment and resources for a wide range of trades.

Ability to focus on one area: Specialized special trades businesses can focus their efforts on one area and become experts in that specific trade.

Easier to manage: These businesses are typically easier to manage because they have a more defined scope of work and require less diverse skills.

Disadvantages:

Limited scope of work: Special trades businesses are limited to their specific trade and may miss out on opportunities to offer additional services to their customers.

Lower profit margins: Special trades businesses may have lower profit margins due to the lower overhead costs but also due to the competitive market where there are other specialized businesses as well as general contractors offering the same services.

Reliant on other businesses: Specialized special trades businesses often rely on general contractors to hire them for projects, which can limit their ability to grow and find new clients.

Lack of flexibility: Special trades businesses may lack the flexibility to offer a wide range of services to their customers, which can limit their ability to take on new projects.

General Contracting Business:

A general contracting business offers a wide range of construction services, and typically acts as the project manager for a construction project. General contractors hire subcontractors to perform specialized work, such as plumbing or electrical installation. Here are some of the advantages and disadvantages of starting a general contracting business:

Advantages:

Higher profit margins: General contractors can charge a markup on the work done by subcontractors, resulting in higher profit margins.

Ability to offer a wide range of services: General contractors can offer a wide range of construction services to their customers, which can result in more opportunities to generate revenue.

Greater flexibility: General contractors have the ability to adapt to changing market conditions and customer needs, which can help them stay competitive.

Potential for growth: General contractors have the potential to grow their business by hiring additional subcontractors and expanding their service offerings.

Disadvantages:

High overhead costs: General contractors typically have higher overhead costs due to the need to invest in equipment and resources for a wide range of trades.

More complex management: General contractors must manage a team of subcontractors, which can be more complex and require diverse skills and knowledge.

More competition: General contracting businesses are more common and there is more competition in the market.

Greater risk: General contractors take on greater risk as they are responsible for managing the entire project and ensuring that the work is completed on time and within budget.

In conclusion, starting a specialized special trades business or a general contracting business each have their own advantages and disadvantages. It's important for entrepreneurs to evaluate their skills and goals, as well as the local

Pro tip:

Consider your skills and experience in the construction industry before choosing between a general contracting business or specialized trades business model. If you have a wide range of skills and experience in various trades, a general contracting business may be a better fit. If you have a specific skill set, such as painting or carpentry, a specialized trades business may be a better option.

Go tip:

Research the market demand in your area for both general contracting and specialized trades businesses. Look for areas where there may be gaps in the market or high demand for certain trades. This can help you determine which business model may be more profitable and successful in your area.

6

FROM CONCEPT TO CONCRETE

Building the Foundation of Your Residential Remodeling Business

Starting a successful remodeling business requires hard work, dedication, and a solid business plan. *Here are some steps you can follow to start your own residential remodeling company:*

Develop a business plan: A business plan outlines your company's goals, target market, marketing strategies, and financial projections. This document is essential for securing funding, attracting investors, and keeping your business on track.

Obtain the necessary licenses and permits: Before you can start working on client projects, you'll need to obtain any necessary licenses and permits. This may include a contractor's license, a building permit, and liability insurance.

Build a team: As your business grows, you'll need to build a team of skilled professionals to handle the workload. This may include carpenters, electricians, plumbers, and designers.

Build a network: Building a network of satisfied clients, suppliers, and industry professionals can help you attract new business and grow your company.

Invest in marketing: To attract new clients, you'll need to invest in marketing your business. This may include creating a website, building a social media presence, and attending industry events.

Provide exceptional customer service: Providing excellent customer service is essential to building a strong reputation and attracting repeat business. Make sure you are responsive, transparent, and deliver high-quality work on time and on budget.

In conclusion, a residential remodeling company is a business that specializes in improving homes. These companies make money by charging clients for their services and may also sell products to clients. By following these steps, you can start your own successful remodeling business and make a name for yourself in the industry.

Pro tip:

For Building a General Contracting Firm: The 5 Key People You Will Need

Project Manager: A project manager is responsible for overseeing all aspects of a project, from start to finish. This includes managing budgets, timelines, and resources, as well as communicating with clients and other professionals in the industry.

Estimator: An estimator is responsible for determining the cost of a project. This includes analyzing project requirements, materials, and labor costs, and creating accurate estimates that reflect the true cost of the project.

Designer: A designer is responsible for creating designs and plans for residential remodels. This includes creating 3D renderings, selecting materials, and working closely with clients to ensure that their vision is brought to life.

Tradespeople: Tradespeople are the skilled professionals who perform the actual work on a project. This may include carpenters, plumbers, electricians, and other professionals with specialized skills.

Office Manager: An office manager is responsible for managing the administrative functions of a contracting firm. This includes managing finances, handling contracts, and ensuring that all paperwork and

7 BUILDING A WINNING TEAM

The Power of Synergy: Building a High-Performing Team That Drives Success

Should I hire in house or only hire subcontractors in the residential remodeling industry. What are the pros and cons to both?

When it comes to building a successful residential remodeling business, deciding whether to hire in-house employees or solely rely on subcontractors can be a difficult decision. Both options have their advantages and disadvantages, so it's important to weigh them carefully before making a final decision.

Hiring In-House Employees

Pros:

Control and Consistency: With in-house employees, you have more control over the quality of work, timing, and overall consistency. You can train them to follow your company's standards and work procedures.

Flexibility: With employees, you have the flexibility to adjust work schedules, prioritize projects, and assign tasks based on your business's current needs.

Long-Term Investment: Investing in your employees can lead to long-term benefits for your business, such as lower costs, higher retention rates, and increased productivity.

Cons:

Higher Costs: Hiring employees means you'll have to pay for their salaries, benefits, and training costs, which can be a significant expense for a new or small business.

Administrative Responsibilities: As an employer, you'll need to handle various administrative responsibilities such as payroll, taxes, insurance, and compliance with labor laws.

Limited Skill Set: Even if you train your employees to perform various tasks, they may not have the same level of expertise as subcontractors who specialize in certain areas.

Hiring Subcontractors

Pros:

Lower Costs: Subcontractors are typically paid per project or hourly rates, which can be more cost-effective than hiring in-house employees.

Specialized Skills: Subcontractors have specific skills and expertise in their respective areas, such as plumbing, electrical work, or cabinetry, which can improve the quality of work.

Less Administrative Work: Since subcontractors are not employees, you don't have to worry about payroll, taxes, or benefits. You simply pay for their services and focus on managing the project.

Cons:

Less Control: With subcontractors, you have less control over their work schedules, quality of work, and timing. This can make it challenging to maintain consistency throughout the project.

Limited Availability: Subcontractors may not always be available when you need them, which can lead to project delays or increased costs if you have to hire someone else.

Lower Loyalty: Subcontractors may not feel as invested in your business as your in-house employees would, so it may be harder to build a long-term relationship.

In Conclusion, both hiring in-house employees and subcontractors have their advantages and disadvantages. Ultimately, it's up to you to decide what works best for your business based on your goals, budget, and project requirements. A hybrid approach is also an option, where you can hire some in-house employees and subcontract out certain tasks.

Pro tip:

For deciding to hire a subcontractor or hire in-house:

Before making a decision on whether to hire a subcontractor or hire in-house, it is important to weigh the pros and cons of each option carefully. Consider the following factors:

Expertise: If the work required for your project requires specialized skills or expertise that your team does not possess, it may be best to hire a subcontractor who has the necessary experience and knowledge. On the other hand, if the work is relatively straightforward and can be completed by your team, it may be more cost-effective to hire in-house.

Timeframe: Consider the timeline for your project. If you have a tight deadline, a subcontractor may be able to complete the work more quickly since they have the resources and manpower to work efficiently. If you have a more flexible timeline, you may have more options for hiring in-house and developing the necessary skills and expertise over time.

Cost: Compare the costs of hiring a subcontractor versus hiring in-house. Subcontractors may charge higher rates, but they are responsible for their own equipment and insurance. Hiring in-house may require more upfront costs for equipment and training, but it may be more cost-effective in the long run.

Risk: Consider the risks associated with each option. Subcontractors may carry their own insurance, but they may also be working on multiple projects simultaneously. In-house hires may require additional training and supervision to ensure that they are following safety protocols and minimizing risk.

Go tip:

For deciding to hire a subcontractor or hire in-house:

When deciding whether to hire a subcontractor or hire in-house, it is important to keep your project goals in mind. If your priority is to complete the project quickly and efficiently, a subcontractor may be the best option. However, if your goal is to build a team that can work together on future projects, hiring in-house may be the better choice.

Ultimately, the decision will depend on your specific needs and circumstances. Consider the expertise required for your project, your timeline, your budget, and your risk tolerance. Whichever option you choose, make sure to communicate your expectations clearly and establish a strong working relationship with your team or subcontractor. This will help ensure that your project is completed on time, on budget, and to your satisfaction.

8 ESTIMATING AND PRICING JOBS

**Beyond the Numbers: Mastering the Art of
Estimating and Pricing for Profitability**

Starting a career in residential remodeling can be both exciting and challenging, especially when it comes to estimating and pricing jobs efficiently. Accurate estimates and pricing are critical to the success of any remodeling project, as they help ensure that the project is completed on time and within budget. In this chapter, we will discuss some tips and strategies for new subcontractors or general contractors to learn how to estimate and price jobs efficiently.

Develop a detailed scope of work: The first step in estimating and pricing a remodeling job is to develop a detailed scope of work. This should include a list of all the tasks that need to be completed, along with the materials and labor required for each task. The scope of work should be as detailed as possible to ensure that you are accounting for all the necessary work and materials.

Use historical data: One of the best ways to estimate and price jobs efficiently is to use historical data from past projects. If you have completed similar projects in the past, you can use this data to help you estimate the time and cost required for the current project. This can help you identify areas where you may be able to save time or money, as well as potential risks or challenges that may require additional time or resources.

Consult with industry experts: Another way to learn how to estimate and price jobs efficiently is to consult with industry experts. This can include other contractors or subcontractors in the residential remodeling business, as well as suppliers and manufacturers. These experts can provide valuable insights into the cost and time required for specific tasks, as well as potential challenges or risks that may arise during the project.

Utilize estimating software: Estimating software can be a valuable tool for new contractors or subcontractors who are just starting in the residential remodeling business. These programs can help you develop accurate estimates quickly and easily, based on historical data, industry standards, and other factors. Some popular estimating software options include ProEst, PlanSwift, and STACK.

Be mindful of profit margins: When pricing jobs, it is important to be mindful of profit margins. While it may be tempting to underbid a project to win the job, this can be a risky strategy that can lead to losses in the long run. Be sure to factor in your labor costs, materials costs, and overhead expenses when pricing a job, as well as a reasonable profit margin to ensure that your business is sustainable.

In conclusion, learning how to estimate and price jobs efficiently is critical for new contractors or subcontractors starting in the residential remodeling business. By developing a detailed scope of work, using historical data, consulting with industry experts, utilizing estimating software, and being mindful of profit margins, new contractors can ensure that their estimates are accurate and their pricing is competitive. This can help set them up for success and help them build a strong reputation in the industry.

Bonus: Here are seven (7) reasons why valuing your time and using change orders is essential for every residential contractor:

Time is Money: Every hour you spend on a project is valuable, and you should be compensated for it. When a customer requests additional work, you need to assess how much time it will take and how much you should charge for it.

Avoid Misunderstandings: With a written change order in place, there is no room for misunderstandings or disputes. Everything is spelled out in black and white, making it clear what work will be done and how much it will cost.

Protect Your Profit Margin: Doing work for free can quickly eat away at your profit margin. With a change order, you can ensure that you are getting paid for every hour you spend on the project, including additional work outside of the original scope.

Manage Customer Expectations: By using change orders, you can manage your customer's expectations by outlining what work will be done and how much it will cost. This helps prevent surprises and keeps everyone on the same page.

Create a Paper Trail: A change order creates a paper trail that can be used in case of disputes or legal issues. This protects both you and the customer and ensures that everything is documented.

Build Trust: By being transparent about your pricing and time, you build trust with your customers. They will appreciate your honesty and professionalism and are more likely to refer you to others.

Know Your Worth: Valuing your time and charging appropriately for it shows that you respect your own worth as a professional. This sets a standard for how others should treat you and your time.

In conclusion, it's crucial to value your time as a residential contractor and use change orders to ensure that you get paid for every hour you spend on a project. By managing your time and money effectively, you can build a successful business and establish yourself as a respected professional in the industry. Remember, always know what your time is worth, charge accordingly, and never

Pro tip:

On learning how to estimate a remodeling project efficiently:

One of the best ways to learn how to estimate a remodeling project efficiently is to start with a small project and gradually work your way up to larger, more complex projects. By starting small, you can learn how to accurately estimate the time and cost required for each task, as well as identify potential risks and challenges. This can help you develop a system for estimating and pricing jobs that can be applied to larger projects in the

Go tip:

On learning how to estimate a remodeling project efficiently:

To learn how to estimate a remodeling project efficiently, it can be helpful to work with an experienced contractor or subcontractor. This can provide you with valuable insights into the best practices for estimating and pricing jobs, as well as provide opportunities for hands-on learning. By working alongside an experienced professional, you can learn how to develop accurate estimates, manage project costs, and identify potential risks and challenges. This can help you build the skills and expertise necessary to

9 BUILDING A BUZZ

Ultimate Guide to Marketing and Advertising Your Remodeling Business

Marketing and advertising are essential components of any successful remodeling business. They help build brand awareness, generate leads, and establish your business as a trusted provider of high-quality remodeling services. In this chapter, we will explore some effective marketing and advertising strategies for remodeling businesses, as well as a pro tip and go tip for building a buzz.

Develop a Strong Brand Identity: The first step in marketing and advertising your remodeling business is to develop a strong brand identity. This includes creating a logo, tagline, and visual elements that communicate your brand's values and personality. Your brand identity should be consistent across all your marketing materials, including your website, social media, and print ads.

Build a Professional Website: A professional website is critical for any remodeling business. Your website should be visually appealing, easy to navigate, and provide clear information about your services, pricing, and past projects. It should also be optimized for search engines to ensure that potential customers can find your business when searching for remodeling services.

Leverage Social Media: Social media is a powerful tool for building brand awareness and engaging with potential customers. Platforms like Facebook, Instagram, and LinkedIn allow you to showcase your past projects, share customer testimonials, and communicate with your followers. You can also use social media advertising to target specific demographics and geographic locations.

Create High-Quality Content: Creating high-quality content is a great way to establish your business as an expert in the remodeling industry. This can include blog posts, infographics, videos, and other forms of content that provide valuable information to potential customers. High-quality content can also help improve your website's search engine rankings, making it easier for customers to find your business online.

Attend Trade Shows and Events: Attending trade shows and events is a great way to network with other professionals in the remodeling industry and showcase your business to potential customers. You can also use these events to learn about new products and trends in the industry, which can help you stay

Pro tip:

For building a buzz

One effective way to build a buzz for your remodeling business is to focus on providing exceptional customer service. Word-of-mouth referrals are one of the most powerful marketing tools available, and happy customers are more likely to recommend your business to friends and family. By focusing on delivering high-quality work and exceptional customer service, you can build a loyal customer base that will help spread the word about your business.

Go tip:

For building a buzz

To build a buzz for your remodeling business, it can be helpful to partner with other local businesses and organizations. For example, you could team up with a local real estate agent to offer home staging services or partner with a home goods store to showcase your past projects. These partnerships can help you reach new audiences and establish your business as a trusted provider of remodeling services in your community.

10 BUILDING A SOLID FOUNDATION

The Importance of Financial Management in the Residential Remodeling Industry

Managing your finances is an essential component of running a successful business in the residential remodeling industry. Without proper financial management, it can be difficult to make informed decisions about pricing, investments, and growth. In this chapter, we will explore some reasons why it is important to manage your finances in the residential remodeling industry.

Maintain profitability: One of the primary reasons to manage your finances in the residential remodeling industry is to maintain profitability. By keeping track of your expenses, revenues, and profit margins, you can identify areas where you may be overspending or undercharging for your services. This can help you adjust your pricing and expenses to ensure that your business remains profitable over the long term.

Make informed decisions: Managing your finances can also help you make informed decisions about investments and growth opportunities. For example, if you are considering expanding your services or opening a new location, you can use financial data to assess the potential costs and benefits of these decisions. This can help you make strategic choices that will help your business grow and thrive.

Monitor cash flow: Monitoring your cash flow is critical for any business, but it is especially important in the residential remodeling industry, where projects often require significant upfront costs. By keeping track of your cash flow, you can ensure that you have the necessary funds to complete projects on time and pay your employees and subcontractors. This can help you avoid cash flow problems that can lead to delays or even bankruptcy.

Prepare for tax season: Managing your finances also helps you prepare for tax season. By keeping accurate records of your expenses, revenues, and other financial data, you can ensure that you are able to file your taxes accurately and on time. This can help you avoid penalties and fees that can result from mistakes or missed deadlines.

Build a strong reputation: Finally, managing your finances can help you build a strong reputation in the residential remodeling industry. By maintaining accurate records and delivering projects on time and within budget, you can establish a reputation as a reliable and trustworthy provider of remodeling services. This can help you attract new customers and build long-term relationships with existing ones.

In conclusion, managing your finances is essential for running a successful business in the residential remodeling industry. By maintaining profitability, making informed decisions, monitoring cash flow, preparing for tax season, and building a strong reputation, you can ensure that your business remains profitable and sustainable over the long term.

Pro tip:

For managing your finances in the residential remodeling business:

One effective way to manage your finances in the residential remodeling business is to create a budget for each project. This can help you track your expenses and ensure that you are staying within your budget. Be sure to include all expenses, including materials, labor, permits, and other costs, and make adjustments as necessary throughout the project to ensure that you are staying on track.

Go tip:

For for managing your finances in the residential remodeling business:

To effectively manage your finances in the residential remodeling business, it can be helpful to work with a financial advisor or accountant. These professionals can help you develop a financial plan, create a budget, and manage your cash flow. They can also provide insights into tax planning, investments, and other financial matters that can help you build a sustainable business.

11 BUILDING BEYOND WALLS

Strategies for Growing Your Residential Remodeling Business

Growing a residential remodeling business can be a challenging task, but it is essential for long-term success. By expanding your services, increasing your customer base, and establishing a strong reputation in the industry, you can take your business to the next level. In this chapter, we will explore some strategies for growing your residential remodeling business.

Expand Your Services: One way to grow your residential remodeling business is to expand your services. For example, if you currently specialize in kitchen and bathroom remodels, you could consider adding services such as basement finishing, outdoor living spaces, or whole-house renovations. This can help you attract new customers and increase revenue from existing ones.

Increase Your Customer Base: Another way to grow your

residential remodeling business is to increase your customer base. This can be done through targeted marketing and advertising campaigns, as well as by offering referral incentives to existing customers. By expanding your reach and attracting new customers, you can increase your revenue and establish a strong reputation in the industry.

Establish Partnerships: Establishing partnerships with other businesses in the residential remodeling industry can also help you grow your business. For example, you could partner with a local supplier of building materials to offer discounted prices to your customers. You could also team up with a real estate agent to offer home staging services, which can help attract potential buyers and increase the value of the home.

Invest in Technology: Investing in technology can also help you grow your residential remodeling business. For example, you could implement project management software to streamline your workflow and improve communication with your team and customers. You could also use 3D modeling software to help your customers visualize their projects before construction begins.

Build a Strong Reputation: Finally, building a strong reputation in the industry is critical for growing your residential remodeling business. This can be done by delivering high-quality work, providing exceptional customer service, and establishing relationships with other professionals in the industry. A strong reputation can help you attract new customers and build long-term relationships

Pro tip:

For growing your residential remodeling business

One effective way to grow your residential remodeling business is to focus on building a loyal customer base. By delivering high-quality work and exceptional customer service, you can establish a reputation as a trusted provider of remodeling services. This can lead to repeat business and word-of-mouth referrals, which are some of the most powerful marketing tools available.

Go tip:

For growing your residential remodeling business:

To grow your residential remodeling business, it can be helpful to network with other professionals in the industry. This can include attending trade shows and events, joining local business associations, and collaborating with other contractors or subcontractors. By building relationships with other professionals in the industry, you can expand your reach and attract new customers who may not have otherwise heard of your business.

CHAPTER

12

CHAPTER

RENOVATING WITH CARE

Avoiding Common Pitfalls in the Residential Remodeling Industry

Operating a residential remodeling business can be a rewarding and profitable endeavor, but it is not without its challenges. In this chapter, we will explore some common pitfalls that remodeling business owners face and how to avoid them

Underestimating project costs: One of the most common pitfalls of operating a residential remodeling business is underestimating project costs. This can lead to cost overruns, which can eat into your profits and damage your reputation. To avoid this pitfall, it is essential to create detailed project plans and budgets that take into account all of the necessary expenses, including labor, materials, permits, and other costs.

Overreliance on a few customers: Another common pitfall is overreliance on a few customers. This can be risky, as losing a few key customers can have a significant impact on your business. To avoid this pitfall, it is important to diversify your customer base and continually seek out new business opportunities.

Inadequate marketing and advertising: Inadequate marketing and advertising can also be a pitfall for remodeling businesses. Without effective marketing and advertising, it can be difficult to attract new customers and establish a strong reputation in the industry. To avoid this pitfall, it is important to develop a comprehensive marketing and advertising strategy that includes both traditional and digital channels.

Poor project management: Poor project management is another common pitfall for remodeling businesses. Without effective project management, projects can become disorganized and lead to delays, cost overruns, and dissatisfied customers. To avoid this pitfall, it is essential to implement project management software and establish clear communication channels with your team and customers.

Inadequate financial management: Finally, inadequate financial management is a common pitfall for remodeling businesses. Without proper financial management, it can be difficult to make informed decisions about pricing, investments, and growth. To avoid this pitfall, it is essential to keep accurate financial records, create budgets and financial plans, and work with a financial advisor or accountant.

Pro tip:

For avoiding common pitfalls

One effective way to avoid common pitfalls is to seek out advice and guidance from other professionals in the industry. This can include joining industry associations, attending trade shows and events, and networking with other remodeling business owners. By learning from the experiences of others, you can gain valuable insights and avoid common pitfalls that could otherwise derail your business.

Go tip:

For avoiding common pitfalls:

To avoid common pitfalls in the residential remodeling industry, it can be helpful to invest in ongoing training and education. This can include attending workshops and seminars, obtaining certifications in specialized areas of remodeling, and staying up-to-date on the latest trends and technologies in the industry. By continually improving your skills and knowledge, you can ensure that your business remains competitive and successful over the long term.

WORDS

"Building Your Dream, One Remodel at a Time: Taking the First Step Towards a Six-Figure Residential Remodeling Business"

In conclusion, starting a six-figure remodeling business can be a challenging yet rewarding endeavor. With dedication, hard work, and a commitment to excellence, you can build a successful business that provides high-quality remodeling services to your customers. However, it is important to be aware of the common pitfalls that many remodeling businesses face, such as underestimating project costs, overreliance on a few customers, poor project management, and inadequate financial management.

To learn more about how to start and grow a successful remodeling business, I encourage you to join the Contractor Envy Community at www.contractorenvy.com. This community provides a wealth of resources and connections to help you build a thriving business, including access to industry experts, educational resources, and networking opportunities.

Additionally, be sure to check out our social media sites and additional books for special trades, which can provide valuable insights and inspiration for your remodeling business. With the right mindset, tools, and resources, you can start a successful six-figure remodeling business today and build a bright future for yourself and your customers.

Pro tip:

For starting today with no excuses:

One effective way to start today with no excuses is to break down your goals into smaller, achievable tasks. Often, the thought of starting a new business can be overwhelming, leading to procrastination and inaction. By breaking down your goals into smaller tasks, you can make progress each day and build momentum towards your ultimate goal.

Go tip:

For starting today with no excuses:

To start today with no excuses, it can be helpful to seek out a mentor or accountability partner. Having someone to provide guidance, support, and accountability can help you stay focused and motivated, even when faced with challenges or setbacks. Additionally, joining a community of like-minded individuals can provide additional resources and support to help you achieve your goals.

WORKBOOK

"Seven (7) questions for someone starting their residential contracting business that will help them start and grow their business successfully"

What services will your residential contracting business offer?

Identify the specific services you will offer, such as kitchen and bathroom renovations, roofing repairs, and landscaping. Define the scope of work for each service and ensure you have the necessary skills, tools, and resources to deliver quality work.

What Services will you provide? Write them down here:

1. ____
2. ____
3. ____
4. ____
5. ____

____
____
____
____
____
____

Who is your target market?

Determine the demographic, geographic, and psychographic characteristics of your ideal customer. Consider factors such as age, income, location, and lifestyle preferences. This will help you tailor your marketing and sales efforts to attract and retain your target market.

What are five factors to consider when identifying your target market? Write down 5 here:

1. ____
2. ____
3. ____
4. ____
5. ____

____

____

____

How will you market and promote your business?

Identify the marketing channels you will use to reach your target audience. This may include online advertising, social media marketing, email marketing, and local print ads. Determine your budget, create a marketing plan, and measure your results to improve your marketing efforts.

What are three (3) factors to consider when determining how to market and promote your business? Write them down here:

1. ____
2. ____
3. ____

____

How will you manage your finances?

Create a budget and track your expenses to ensure you have enough cash flow to cover your costs and make a profit. Consider hiring an accountant or bookkeeper to help you manage your finances and stay on top of taxes, invoices, and payroll.

How will you manage your finances? Will you hire an accountant or do it yourself. Research your options of management software and systems and Write them down here:

1. ____
2. ____
3. ____
4. ____
5. ____

____

____

How will you manage your team and subcontractors?

Determine the roles and responsibilities of each team member and subcontractor, and create a system for communication, scheduling, and performance management. Provide training and feedback to help your team improve their skills and meet your business goals.

Who will you need to hire in house or as a subcontractor? Write them down here:

1. ____
2. ____
3. ____
4. ____
5. ____

____

____

How will you manage your projects?

Create a project management system that tracks the progress of each project, identifies potential issues, and ensures that deadlines are met. Communicate with clients regularly to keep them informed of the project's status and address any concerns.

Will you be using a CRM program such as BuilderTrend or CoConstruct, etc? Decide on an invoicing system and CRM and Write them down here:

1. ____
2. ____
3. ____
4. ____
5. ____

____

How will you ensure customer satisfaction?

Develop a customer service strategy that emphasizes quality workmanship, clear communication, and timely response to inquiries and complaints. Monitor customer feedback and reviews to identify areas for improvement and make changes to your business operations as necessary.

How will you maintain great customer service? Write them down here:

1. ____
2. ____
3. ____
4. ____
5. ____

____
____
____
____

Sure, here's a workbook with a checklist of things to do to start your residential remodeling business today:

Research your market

-     Identify the competition in your area and assess their strengths and weaknesses
-     Determine the demand for your services by conducting market research and analyzing demographic data

Who is your target Market? Write down the top 5 here:

1. ____
2. ____
3. ____
4. ____
5. ____

____
____
____
____

Develop a business plan

- Define your services and target market
- Create a budget and financial projections
- Determine your pricing strategy
- Develop a marketing plan

Write down notes here for your business plan:

____

____

____

____

____

____

____

____

____

____

____

____

____

____

____

____

____

____

____

____

____

____

____

____

Register your business

☐ Choose a business name and register it with the appropriate state agency

☐ Obtain any required licenses and permits

☐ Register for a tax identification number and any necessary business taxes

Write down a checklist for accomplishing registering your business and check it off as you complete these tasks:

1. Choose Business Name: _______________________________________

2. Register it with the State Agency

3. Obtain required licenses-What licenses do you need? Write down here:

____

____

4. Register Business with irs.gov to get free Employer Identification Number (EIN)

Establish a legal structure for your business

- ☐ Choose a legal structure, such as a sole proprietorship, partnership, LLC, or corporation
- ☐ Consult with an attorney to ensure you're following all legal requirements

Set up your business operations

- ☐ Choose a location for your business and set up an office or workspace
- ☐ Purchase or lease any necessary equipment or tools
- ☐ Hire any necessary employees or contractors

Answer these questions:

Will you need a location? And if so, Why? Write down here:

____

____

What tools are needed to start? Write down here:

____

____

Develop a website and online presence

- ☐ Create a website that showcases your services, past projects, and customer reviews
- ☐ Establish a presence on social media and other relevant platforms to reach potential customers

What social site will you establish your presence? Write down here:

____

____

Set up you're bookkeeping and accounting systems

☐   Choose a bookkeeping software and set up your accounts

☐   Hire an accountant or bookkeeper to manage your finances and help you file taxes

What software will you use to manage your business? Write down here:

Develop a project management system

☐ Create a system for managing projects from start to finish, including budgeting, scheduling, and client communication

Write down three (3) software programs you have reviewed that will help you manage your business:

Obtain insurance coverage

☐ Purchase liability insurance to protect your business and your clients in case of accidents or property damage

What insurance do you think you need? Call an insurance agent today and ask what insurance you will need. Write your notes here:

Network and build relationships

☐ Attend industry events and join professional associations to network and build relationships with other contractors, suppliers, and potential clients

Write down (3) Events you will attend in the next 3 months here:

1.____

2.____

3.____

By completing this checklist and workbook, you'll be well on your way to starting your residential remodeling business. Good luck! I hope these questions help you start and grow your residential contracting business successfully.

GOOD LUCK!

ABOUT THE AUTHOR

Kevin Starks is a licensed class B general contractor with years of experience in the residential remodeling industry. He currently works as a full-time project manager at Strategic Remodel Inc, a high-end remodeling company located in Wichita, Kansas. Kevin's educational background includes multiple vocational degrees in building trades, cabinetry, and welding, as well as completing a 4,000-hour apprenticeship for Journeyman Carpentry from the State of California.

In addition to his work at Strategic Remodel Inc, Kevin is the owner of Widerange Builders, a company that invests in fix-and-hold projects and ground-up construction. He has also launched "Contractor Envy," a community for the residential remodeling industry that provides resources and support for those in the field or entering the field. Kevin's future goals include becoming a residential remodeling influencer and helping to improve the industry with proper training systems and business structures.

Kevin has been in the residential remodeling industry for years and has a wealth of knowledge and experience to share. He decided to write "How to Start a Six Figure Remodeling Contracting Business" to help others who are interested in starting their own successful remodeling business. With practical tips and insights, Kevin's book is a must-read for anyone looking to enter the industry or take their business to the next level.

In addition to his book, Kevin also hosts the Contractor Envy Presents The Nail It Podcast. Listeners can tune in to learn from Kevin's expert advice and gain valuable insights from his guests.

Kevin's passion for the industry and his desire to help others succeed doesn't stop there. He has a new book coming out called "Nailed It," which gives readers a glimpse into his personal life and his journey on starting his own business after experiencing failure. This book is sure to inspire and motivate readers to push through their own challenges and achieve success.

Overall, Kevin Starks is dedicated to helping others succeed in the remodeling industry. Whether through his book, podcast, or personal story, he is committed to sharing his knowledge and expertise to help others achieve their goals.

Interested in becoming part of the Contractor Envy Community please follow and subscribe to the channel on Youtube, Facebook, Instagram and Tiktok. We promise nothing but valuable information and entertainment.